My Sticker Book of
Travel Fun

Claire Watts

How to use this book
Here is a sticker book full of fun puzzles and games
to keep you busy in the car and in your hotel room
on both long and short trips.
To complete the pages you will need felt-tip pens,
pencils, or crayons, and thin cardboard for the games.
Many of the puzzles can be solved with stickers, which you
will find on the middle two pages of the book.
Answers to all the questions appear on page 16.

The following symbols are used in this book:

 The gray circle symbol
means there is a sticker
to put here on the page.

 Wherever a written
answer is needed, there is
a colored box to fill in.

DK PUBLISHING, INC.

Packing

Get packing

Jane is packing her suitcase to go on a beach vacation, and Mark is packing his suitcase to go on a ski vacation. All their things have been mixed up. Can you sort out which clothes and objects each of them will need to take?

Mark's suitcase

Write in the boxes the number of items each child packs.

Jane's suitcase

puzzles

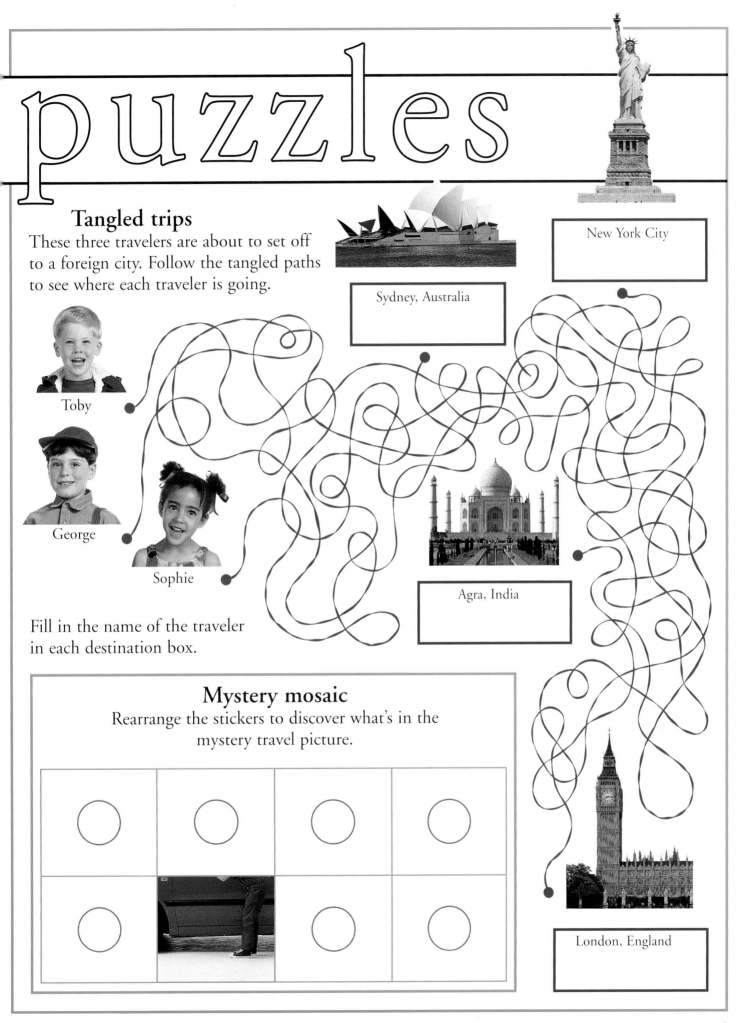

Tangled trips

These three travelers are about to set off to a foreign city. Follow the tangled paths to see where each traveler is going.

Toby

George

Sophie

Fill in the name of the traveler in each destination box.

Sydney, Australia

New York City

Agra, India

London, England

Mystery mosaic

Rearrange the stickers to discover what's in the mystery travel picture.

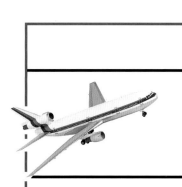

Travel

Use this chart to keep a record of four special trips. Fill in the chart as you travel.

You can also try your hand at solving the fantastic trip puzzle below.

	Destination and date Write in where you are going and the date.	Departure time Draw in clock hands and circle day or night.	Forms of transportation Circle each type of transportation you use on your journey.
Trip 1	To...... From...... Date......		
Trip 2	To...... From...... Date......		
Trip 3	To...... From...... Date......		
Trip 4	To...... From...... Date......		

Fantastic journey

Imagine you are going on a magical trip during which you see some amazing animals. Study the clues opposite then use your stickers to put the creatures you see in the correct order on the map.

• The lizard is not the first thing you see.

• You see the whale right after the giraffe.

• The third thing you spot is a giraffe.

• You see the lizard before you spot the giraffe.

• You see the elephant and the whale before the dinosaur.

tracker

My favorite trip was

Once you have completed the chart, record the details of your favorite journey in the notebook above.

Travelling companions Fill in how many people are traveling with you.	Food and snacks Circle what you eat and drink along the way.	Arrival time Draw in clock hands, and circle day or night	Travel time Fill in how long the trip took.	Distance Fill in how far you traveled.
			..............hours ....minutes	.... miles/kilometers
			..............hours ....minutes	.... miles/kilometers
			..............hours ....minutes	.... miles/kilometers
			..............hours ....minutes	.... miles/kilometers

2   4

3   5

Car collectors

Can you spot 20 cars of the same color in an hour? Each time you do, add the correct car sticker to the traffic jam.

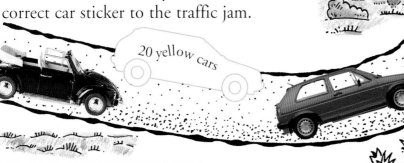

20 yellow cars

20 blue cars

Look closer

This is a close-up of part of a vehicle on these pages. Figure out which one and write its name below.

. . . .

Traveler's wheel

Play this eye-opening game when you travel by car or bus. The goal is to spot 16 of the 21 objects, including a police car, in one journey. Check off each object as you see it. Use one ring of boxes for each trip.

I spy game

The goal of this game is to guess the object that your opponent is looking at while you are traveling.

I spy, with my little eye, something beginning with T.

The player who guesses the object picks next.

Count up!

How many land vehicles can you count on these pages? Write the answer in the box.

challenge

20 green cars

20 red cars

3 7 9

Spot the number

Look for every number from
1 to 100, in the right order, during
your journey. Write the number you
count to in this box.

Hide-and-seek

Peter's suitcase has burst open on the bus trip.
Can you find 10 lost things hidden in the
picture? Color in each object as you find it.

Amazing!

Welcome to Mazeville! Unfortunately there's chaos everywhere, and many of the streets are closed off.

Can you direct your taxi through the twisting streets from the Grand Hotel to the train station, avoiding all the obstacles? Good luck!

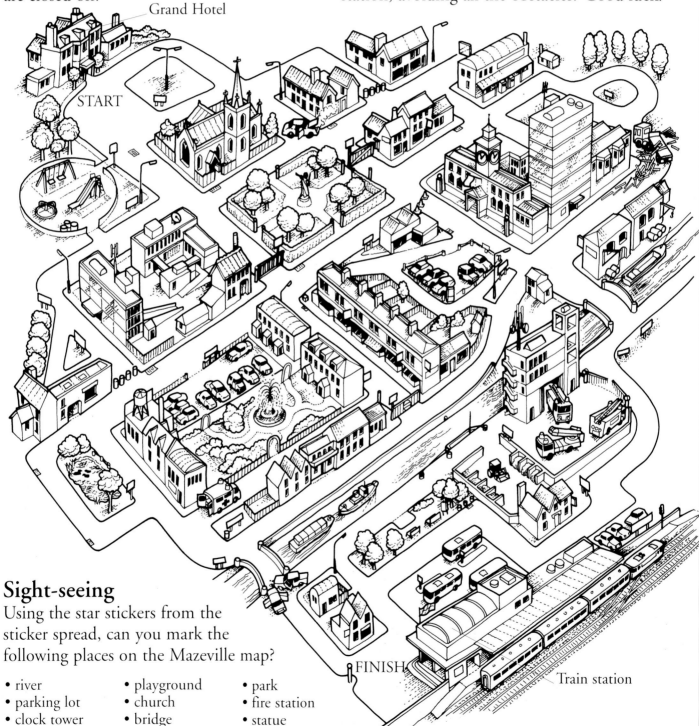

Grand Hotel

START

FINISH

Train station

Sight-seeing
Using the star stickers from the sticker spread, can you mark the following places on the Mazeville map?

- river
- parking lot
- clock tower
- playground
- church
- bridge
- park
- fire station
- statue

Stickers

Page 3

Pages 4/5

Pages 6/7

Page 8

Page 11

Pages 14/15

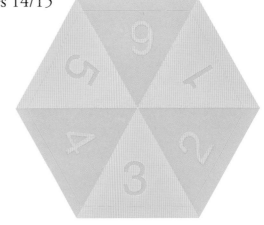

Pages 12/13

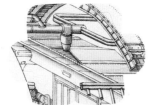

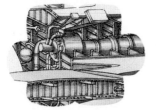

Act it out

Rock, paper, scissors

Both players start with one hand behind them. On the count of three, you both bring out a hand formed into one of these signs:

Paper

Scissors

Rock

Compare the signs and score as follows:
• Scissors cut paper – win 10 points.
• Paper covers rock – win 10 points.
• Rock blunts scissors – win 10 points.
If you both make the same sign, no one scores. The first player to score 50 points wins.

Expressions

Players take turns acting out an emotion using facial expressions. No speaking or hand movement is allowed! Whoever guesses the emotion acts next. The first person to guess three emotions wins.

Look for the expression stickers on the sticker page and match them to the words below. Can you act each one out?

○

Happy

○

Angry

What a noise!

The goal of this game is to be as silly and noisy as you can. Before you start, complete the set of pictures below by matching the animal stickers to the right captions. Whenever you pass any of the animals or objects below on your trip, everyone has to make the right sound and action. Think up others as you go.

○ Flap your arms around and shout "Quack, quack!"

  Pedal your arms and shout "Ding-a-ling!"

  Pretend to drive and shout "Beep, beep!"

○ Put your hands on your head for horns and shout "Moo!"

  Sit up and beg and shout "Woof, woof!"

  Wave and shout "Vrrmm, vrrmm!"

Scribble art

Can you make pictures out of scribbles?
First look at the example below,
then try drawing on the
scribbles opposite.

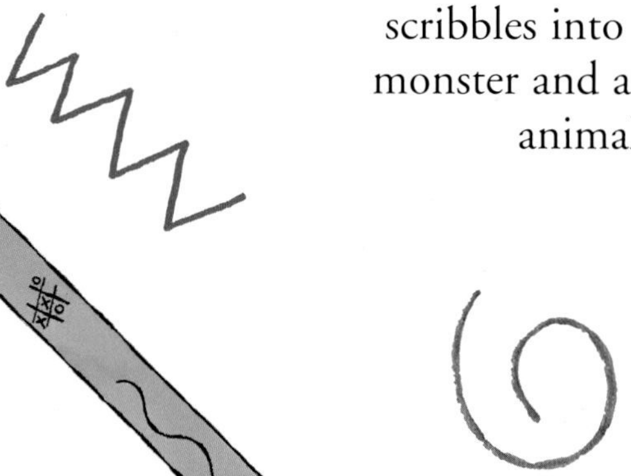

Now draw your own
scribble pictures
in the box.

Can you turn these
scribbles into a
monster and an
animal?

Tic-tac-toe

This is a game for
two players – one
player draws Os and the
other draws Xs. Each player
takes turns marking an O or
an X in one of the grid squares.
The first person to make a vertical,
horizontal, or diagonal line of three is
the winner. If no one makes a line, the
game is a draw.

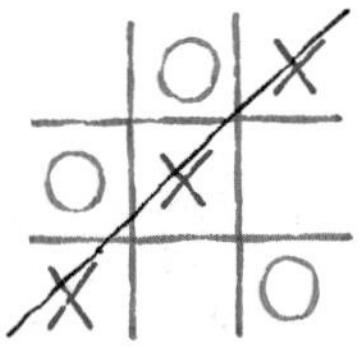

In this example,
X is the
winner.

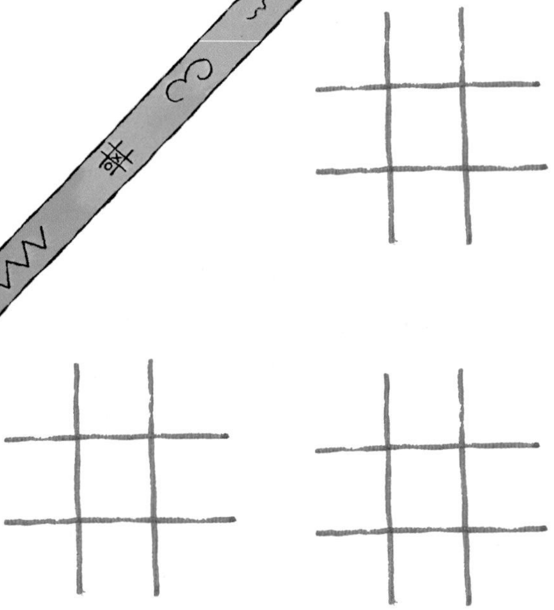

If you use a pencil on these pages you can erase the writing and play the games again.

Making the shapes spinner

1. Stick the shapes spinner sticker on cardboard and cut it out.
2. Ask an adult to push a used toothpick through the center.
3. To use, spin your spinner on a flat surface. When it stops, the shape touching the surface is the chosen one.

Spin a shape

Spin the spinner four times to select four shapes. Ask someone to act as judge. Players have to try to draw pictures, using these four shapes, in the blank box below. You can use each shape as many times as you like. The winner is the player who draws the best picture.

Beetle game

Players take turns spinning the shapes spinner and drawing a part of a beetle's body. Use the key opposite as a guide for how many of each part is needed. You must spin a body to start, then a head before you can draw the face and antennae. If you spin a body part you don't need, you miss a turn. The winner is the first player to complete a beetle picture.

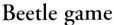

KEY
The beetle needs:

■	body	draw 1
●	head	draw 1
▲	leg	draw 6
★	tail	draw 1
▬	face	draw 1
☾	antenna	draw 2

11

Jumbo jigsaw

Here's your chance to take a fascinating look behind the scenes of a jumbo jet, but you will need to finish the jigsaw puzzle first. Look on the sticker page for the missing pieces. Decide where each piece goes before you stick it on, since you can't move it if it's wrong!

Plane spotting

Look carefully at the picture. Can you find everything listed below? Check each thing off as you spot it.

1   Someone going to bed

2   Someone in a striped shirt

3   A radar dish

4   Two people reading newspapers

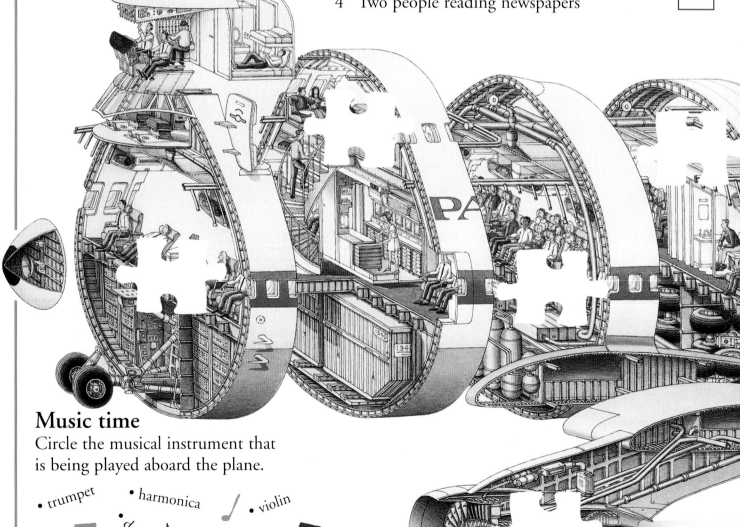

Music time

Circle the musical instrument that is being played aboard the plane.

- trumpet
- harmonica
- violin
- drum
- piano
- tuba
- flute

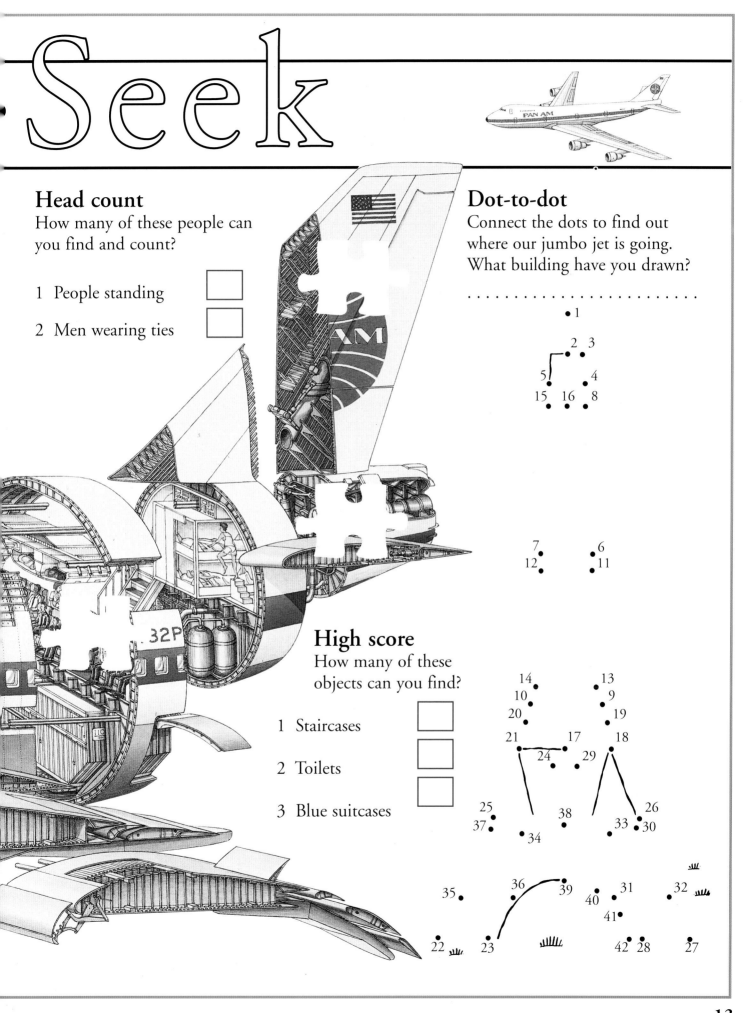

Seek

Head count
How many of these people can you find and count?

1 People standing ☐

2 Men wearing ties ☐

Dot-to-dot
Connect the dots to find out where our jumbo jet is going. What building have you drawn?

. . . .

High score
How many of these objects can you find?

1 Staircases ☐

2 Toilets ☐

3 Blue suitcases ☐

Egyptian

Who will win this race through ancient Egypt to find the hidden treasure in the pyramid?

You will need
• Thin cardboard • A toothpick • Game counters and spinner stickers • Scissors

Making the game pieces
1. Stick the four character counters and spinner onto cardboard and cut them out.*
2. Ask an adult to push a toothpick through the center of the spinner.

Playing the game
• Players place their chosen counters at the start.
• Take turns spinning the spinner. You need to spin an odd number to start, then spin again and move the number of spaces shown.
• Watch out for the hazards along the way.
• Players must spin the exact number needed to finish.
• The winner is the first person to enter the pyramid.

Puzzling pictures
Study the ancient Egyptian writing called hieroglyphics. Find the six stickers and place them below. Can you figure out which two are the same?

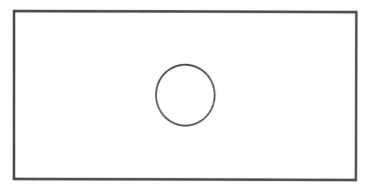

Hitch ride with camel train. Move ahead 5 spaces.

Stop at oasis for fresh water. Miss a turn.

*Ask an adult to help you with this.

adventure

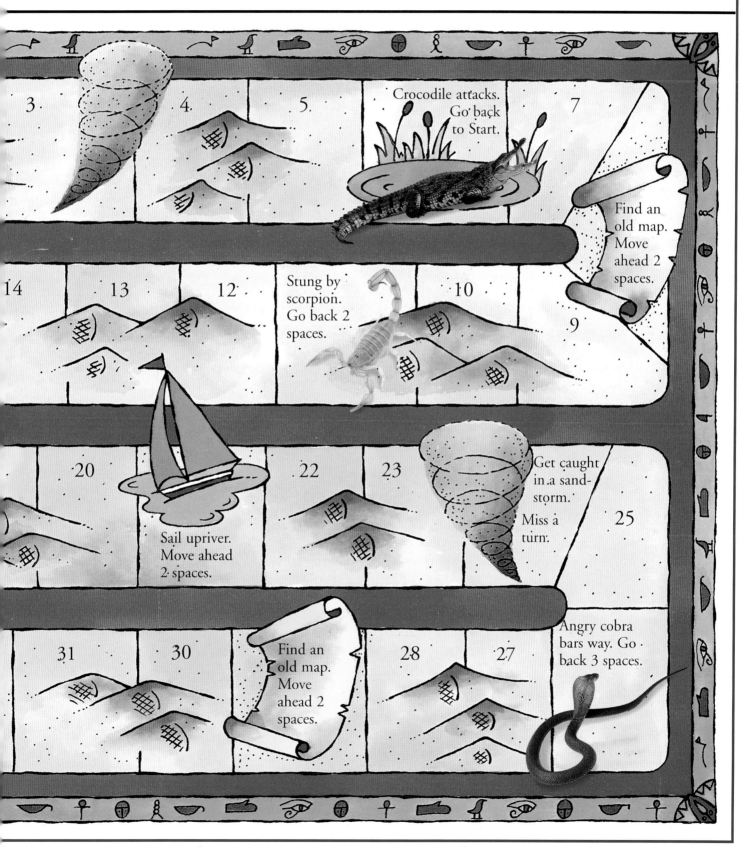

3

4

5

Crocodile attacks. Go back to Start.

7

Find an old map. Move ahead 2 spaces.

14

13

12

Stung by scorpion. Go back 2 spaces.

10

9

20

Sail upriver. Move ahead 2 spaces.

22

23

Get caught in a sandstorm. Miss a turn.

25

31

30

Find an old map. Move ahead 2 spaces.

28

27

Angry cobra bars way. Go back 3 spaces.

Answers

Pages 2/3 Packing puzzles
Get packing
Jane takes 7 things.
Mark takes 8 things.
Tangled trips
Toby went to Agra, Sophie went to New York,
George went to Sydney, no one went to London.
Mystery mosaic

Pages 4/5 Travel tracker
Fantastic trip
1 Elephant, 2 Lizard, 3 Giraffe, 4 Whale, 5 Dinosaur.

Pages 6/7 Traveler's challenge
Look closer
Red tractor.
Count up!
27 land vehicles (not including stickers).
Hide and seek

1 book	6 swim ring
2 bucket	7 shorts
3 fishing rod	8 spade
4 flippers	9 tennis racket
5 kite	10 vest

Page 8 Amazing!

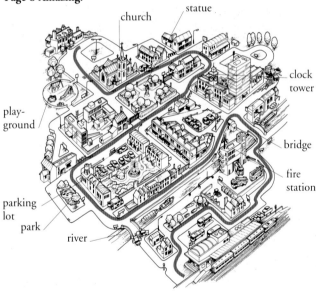

Pages 12/13 Hide and seek
Music time
Piano
Head count
People standing 5 Men wearing ties 10
Dot-to-dot
Eiffel Tower, Paris, France
High score
Staircases 2, Toilets 1,
Blue suitcases 3

Pages 14/15 Egyptian adventure
Puzzling pictures
These hieroglyphics appear twice.

A DK PUBLISHING BOOK

Editor Helen Drew
Assistant Editor Sarah Johnston
Design Sheilagh Noble and Sarah Cowley
DTP Designer Almudena Díaz
Jacket design Mark Haygarth

Managing Editor Jane Yorke
Managing Art Editor Chris Scollen
US Editor Kristin Ward
Production Ruth Cobb

Illustrations by Sally Kindberg and John Hutchinson
Photography by Sarah Ashun, Gordon Clayton,
Andy Crawford, Mike Dunning, Steve Gorton, Dave King,
Bob Langrish, Richard Leeny, Michael Morian,
Stephen Oliver, Susanna Price, Steve Shott, Alan Williams.

First American Edition, 1997
2 4 6 8 10 9 7 5 3 1
Published in the United States by DK Publishing, Inc.
95 Madison Avenue, New York, New York 10016

Visit us on the World Wide Web at http://www.dk.com

Copyright © 1997 Dorling Kindersley Limited, London

Photography (Taj Mahal, page 3) copyright © 1992 Chris Branfield.
Photography (camel, page 15) copyright © 1991 Phillip Dowell.
Photography (horned toad, sticker page; Nile crocodile, sticker page; rough
collie, sticker page) copyright © 1990, 1991, 1991 Jerry Young.

ISBN 0-7894-1525-9

Color reproduction by Colourscan, Singapore
Printed and bound in Italy by Graphicom.